D0508802

Get Active!

Louise Spilsbury

Published 2009 by
A & C Black Publishers Ltd.
36 Soho Square, London, W1D 3QY
www.acblack.com

ISBN HB 978-1-4081-0850-5
    PB 978-1-4081-1297-7

Series consultant: Gill Matthews

Text copyright © 2009 Louise Spilsbury

The right of Louise Spilsbury to be identified as the author of this work has been asserted by her in accordance with the Copyrights, Designs and Patents Act 1988.

A CIP catalogue for this book is available from the British Library.

All rights reserved. No part of this publication may be reproduced in any form or by any means – graphic, electronic or mechanical, including photocopying, recording, taping or information storage and retrieval systems – without the prior permission in writing of the publishers.

Every effort has been made to trace copyright holders and to obtain their permission for use of copyright material. The authors and publishers would be pleased to rectify any error or omission in future editions.

This book is produced using paper that is made from wood grown in managed, sustainable forests. It is natural, renewable and recyclable. The logging and manufacturing processes conform to the environmental regulations of the country of origin.

Produced for A & C Black by Calcium.
Printed and bound in China by C&C Offset Printing Co.

All the internet addresses given in this book were correct at the time of going to press. The author and publishers regret any inconvenience caused if addresses have changed or sites have ceased to exist, but can accept no responsibility for any such changes.

Acknowledgements
The publishers would like to thank the following for their kind permission to reproduce their photographs:
Cover: Shutterstock. **Pages:** Fotolia: Michael Chamberlin 19; Shutterstock: Photocreo Michal Bednarek 5, Linda Bucklin 7, Jacek Chabraszewski 10, 20, Vince Clements 14, Stephen Coburn 16–17, Sonya Etchison 21, Mandy Godbehear 8, 18, Gregory Kendall 17, John Lumb 6, Monkey Business Images 4–5, Paulaphoto 12–13, Julián Rovagnati 15, Suzanne Tucker 13.
Illustration: Geoff Ward 11.

Contents

Why You Should Get Active

If you leave your bike in the garage too long it goes rusty and the tyres go flat. Your body is a bit like that too. You need to use it often to keep it working properly. If you sit around all day you will become unfit.

Being active is a great way to make new friends or to have fun with old friends!

There are lots of reasons to get active:
- It makes you feel good
- It makes you healthy and strong
- It gives you **energy**
- It stops you becoming overweight

What's it all about?

This book will show you how being active helps your body. We'll suggest different kinds of exercise to try. If you follow the tips in this book and get active, you will feel good, look good, and be healthy.

Being active helps you sleep better. This is important because your body needs rest at night to help you keep going in the day.

Building Muscles and Bones

When you are active your **muscles** and **bones** get bigger and stronger.

On the move

Bones are hard and strong. They form the **skeleton** that holds your body up. Bones are attached to muscles. Muscles are stretchy. They pull on the bones to make the bones move. When the bones move, your body moves!

Gymnasts are very flexible. Being active will help to keep your body **supple** so you can bend and twist.

Work that body

When you are young your bones are growing. This is how you get taller. You need to grow strong bones to support your growing body. Strong muscles can keep working for longer. Strong muscles are less likely to get injured.

Without the bones and muscles inside your body you would be as wobbly as a jelly and you would not be able to move!

Did you know?
There are 27 bones in one human hand and 14 in the face!

Exercise is Good for Your Heart

Put your hand on your chest.
Can you feel your **heart** beating?
Your heart is a muscle that moves.
Like any other muscle, the heart needs
to be active to stay strong and healthy.

Healthy hearts

You need a healthy heart because the
heart has a vital job to do. The heart pumps
blood around your body. Blood carries food
and **oxygen** (air) to the rest of the body.
The body uses food and oxygen to make
energy. Energy allows the body to keep
working and to build and repair itself.

Doing activities that make
you hot and out of breath
are great for your heart.
Bouncing on a trampoline is
fun and really good for you.

Make your heart race

The best exercises for the heart are those that make the heart beat faster. Why not try running, dancing, jumping, playing football, or cycling? Keep going until you feel your heart beat faster!

This chart shows **heartbeat** before, during, and just after exercise. When is the heart working hardest?

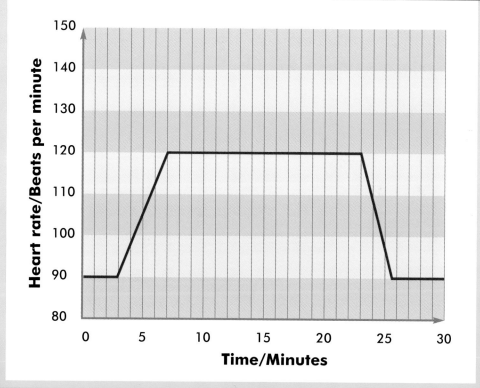

Which Foods Help You To Be Active?

Have you seen those adverts for sports drinks and bars? You don't really need these things for energy when you work out. A healthy, balanced diet will give your body all the energy it needs.

Eating for energy

You need to get active for a healthy body. But activity and exercise require fuel. **Carbohydrates** are foods that the body can easily use for energy. Healthy carbohydrates come from fruits, vegetables, and foods made from grains, such as rice, pasta, and bread.

If you want to be active, eat foods such as pasta and rice. They give you lots of energy.

Eat well

You need to eat different kinds of food. You should eat mostly fruit, vegetables and grain foods. You should also eat some milk and dairy foods, and some meat, fish, eggs, and beans. You should only eat a small amount of foods and drinks that are high in fat or sugar.

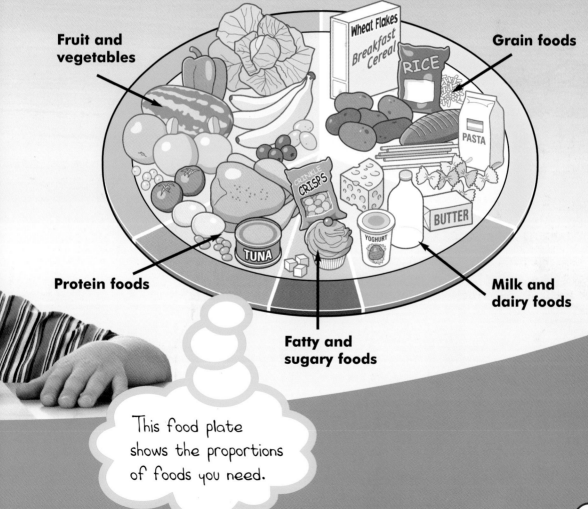

Fruit and vegetables

Grain foods

Protein foods

Milk and dairy foods

Fatty and sugary foods

This food plate shows the proportions of foods you need.

Why You Need To Drink More Water

Your body is about two-thirds water. There is water in your blood, your skin, your **brain** – in fact all over your body. When you don't get enough water you get **dehydrated**. You may feel tired, dizzy, and weak.

Drink and sport

When you are active you sweat more. Sweat is your body's way of cooling down. Water from inside the body comes through tiny holes onto the skin's surface. When this dries in the air it takes some body heat with it, so you feel cooler. To replace this water, drink before, during, and after exercise.

You don't just get water from drinks. You can get some of the water you need from juicy fruits.

Why not be active with water as well as drinking water when you're active?

Did you know?
You need to drink about eight glasses of water a day to keep your body topped up.

Why Should You Wear a Helmet?

Why do you think helmets and pads are called safety gear? Because they keep you safe, of course! Rock climbers and hockey players wear helmets to protect their heads in case of a fall or knock. You should wear the right gear when you are active, too.

A bad fall can break the bones and bruise or strain the muscles inside your body, so you should wear pads for protection.

Use your head

Helmets protect the brain inside your **skull.**
Your brain is the body's control centre. Without it
you cannot survive, so a helmet can save your life.

Get a grip

Some sports gear helps you
to be active! Trainers have
treads that grip the ground
so you can run and change
direction quickly. Stretchy
clothes like leotards or
swimming costumes allow
you to move more easily.

Football boots
have studs to
grip muddy fields.

Why Do Warm-Ups Matter?

Have you ever had sore legs after sport? Or hurt yourself in a game? You should try doing warm-ups! Warm-ups are gentle exercises you do before being active. Doing five to ten minutes of warm-ups reduces the risk of soreness and injury.

How warm-ups work

Warm-ups increase the supply of blood to your muscles. This makes the muscles warm and gives them more energy. That means they are able to move more easily.

Does your team do warm-ups before a match?

Ways to warm up

- Brisk walking
- Skipping
- Slow jogging on the spot
- Stretching and bending
- Toe touches

Cool down

You should always make sure that you cool down after exercise. Cool-downs will help to prevent your legs from becoming sore or stiff later. Why not try stretching your muscles, walking, or jogging on the spot?

Runners usually jog for a few minutes after a race. This helps them cool down and allows their heartbeat to get back to normal gently.

What Exercise is Best?

The best exercise is the one you like most. If exercise isn't fun, it's hard to keep it up. There are loads of activities that you can try to see which you like best.

Give it a go

Why not try a new sport? Just think what fun it would be to join a netball or football team. Or maybe you would prefer an activity where you stretch and bend, like gymnastics or dancing. Trying a new activity will boost your confidence!

It doesn't matter whether you like team sports or exercising alone. The important thing is to be active!

Mix it up

Try doing a mix of activities to exercise all the different parts of the body.

- Rowing and tennis are good for your arm muscles.
- Running and bike-riding are good for your leg muscles.
- Swimming helps many muscles at once.

Don't miss out on that great feeling you get when your team plays well. Get active and join in!

How Often Should You Exercise?

You should exercise for at least an hour every day. But you should be active during the rest of the day too. Try to avoid spending too long in front of the TV or computer. You don't want to become a couch potato, do you?

> If you find it hard to make time to be active, try walking part of the way to school.

Exercising every day helps you to:

- Feel happy and look good
- Sleep soundly
- Build strong bones and muscles
- Stay at a healthy weight

What counts?

It is not just exercise classes and sports that count as exercise. You can be active by helping round the house. Why not try cleaning the car or sweeping the yard?

Now you know why you need to be fit to stay healthy, stop reading this book and get active!

Taking the dog for a walk will make you fit and your family will thank you for it, too!

Glossary

blood red liquid found in tiny tubes called blood vessels inside the
body. It carries food and oxygen

bones the hard parts in the body that make up the skeleton

brain the part of the body found inside the head. It controls the
rest of the body

carbohydrates types of food that provide energy. Rice and pasta
are types of carbohydrate

dehydrated to be without enough water to work properly

energy allows people to do everything they need to live, grow,
and be active. We get energy from the food we eat

heart a muscle that squeezes to pump blood all around the tubes
inside the body

heartbeat the beat of the heart muscle pumping again and again

muscles parts of the body that allow you to move

oxygen a gas in the air around us, necessary to keep us alive

skeleton the framework of bones that gives your body its shape

skull the set of bones that forms your head and protects
the brain

supple able to bend easily

Further Information

Websites

There are ideas for activities as well as facts about why it is important to be active at:

www.childrenfirst.nhs.uk/kids/health/eat_smart/ exercise_centre/index.html

You can choose workouts to do with Sportacus at:
www.bbc.co.uk/cbeebies/lazytown

Find out more about what makes exercise cool at:
http://kidshealth.org/kid/stay_healthy/fit/work_it_out.html

Books

Look After Yourself: Get Some Exercise! by Angela Royston. Heinemann Library (2004).

Exercise and Play (Health Choices) by Cath Senker. Wayland (2004).

Exercise (Health & Fitness) by Judy Sadgrove. Raintree (2000).

Index